The Secret Cave

Story by Annette Smith
Illustrations by Meredith Thomas

Dad stopped the car
at a camp ground by a lake.

Katie and Joe were staying with him
for the weekend.

"This looks like a good place
to camp," said Joe.
"We can go swimming and fishing."

"Look!" said Katie.
"There is a secret cave
   down that trail!   Can we go down it?"

"No, Katie," said Dad.
"We have to put the tent up first.
   Remember, you are not to go away
   by yourself."

Joe helped Dad put up the tent.
Katie helped get the bags
and other things out of the car.
They all worked hard.

Then Dad said to Joe,
"Where is Katie?"

"She's not in here," said Joe,
looking in the tent.
"And she's not in the car."

SECRET CAVE

Joe and Dad looked everywhere,
but they couldn't find Katie.

"I hope she didn't go down that trail
by herself to find the cave," said Dad.
"We had better go down there."

"It will be getting dark soon,"
said Joe.

Katie **had** gone down the trail.
She had gone off by herself
to find the secret cave.
The trail was wet and muddy.

After Katie had walked a little way,
she found the cave
near the side of the trail.
Katie looked inside.
It was dark.
But then she saw something.

Just then, Dad and Joe
came running down the trail.
"**Katie!**" cried Dad.

"We have been looking everywhere
for you," said Joe.

"I'm sorry," said Katie.
"I was just going to walk a little way
down the trail.
Look! I have found the **cave**.
Come and see!
There's a secret inside it!"

13

They went inside the cave.

"Look at the little lights
all over the walls," said Katie.

"Sh-sh-sh!" said Dad.
"They are glowworms.
They have little lights
on the ends of their tails.
We must be very quiet
or they will put their lights out."

"The glowworms are a good secret,"
said Katie.
"Can we come and see them again?"

"Yes, Katie," said Dad, giving her a hug.
"But remember, you must never go away
by yourself again. You did scare me."

"I'm sorry, Dad," said Katie.
"I won't forget."